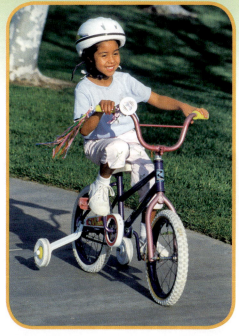

By Kari Capone

Scott Foresman
is an imprint of

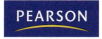

Glenview, Illinois • Boston, Massachusetts • Chandler, Arizona •
Upper Saddle River, New Jersey

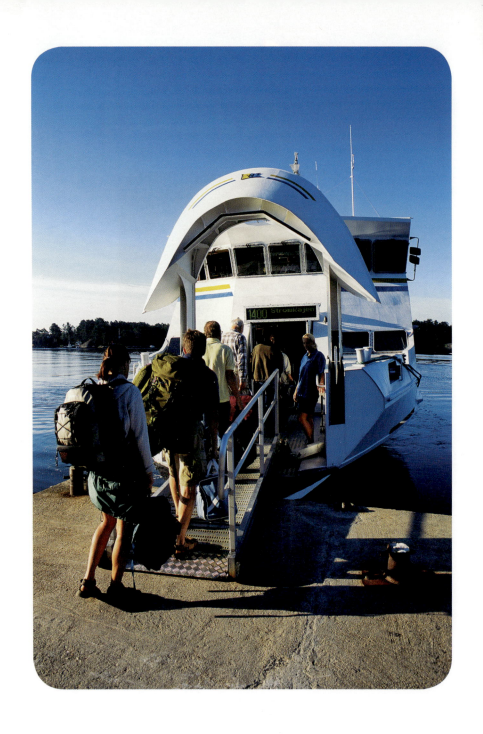

I see a boat.

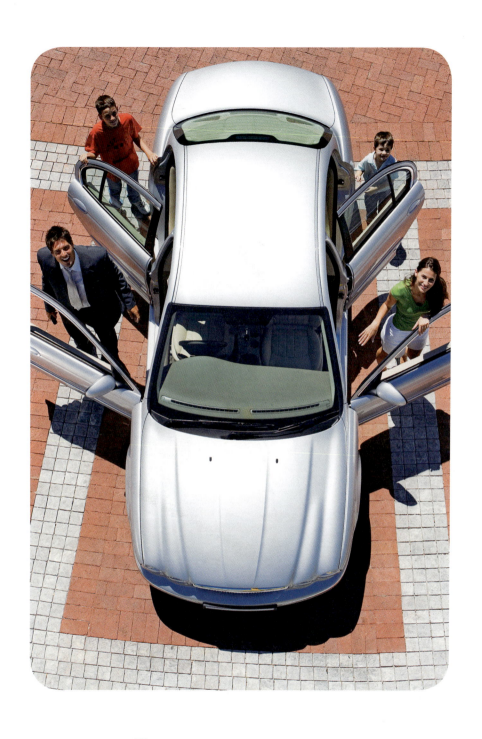

I see a car.

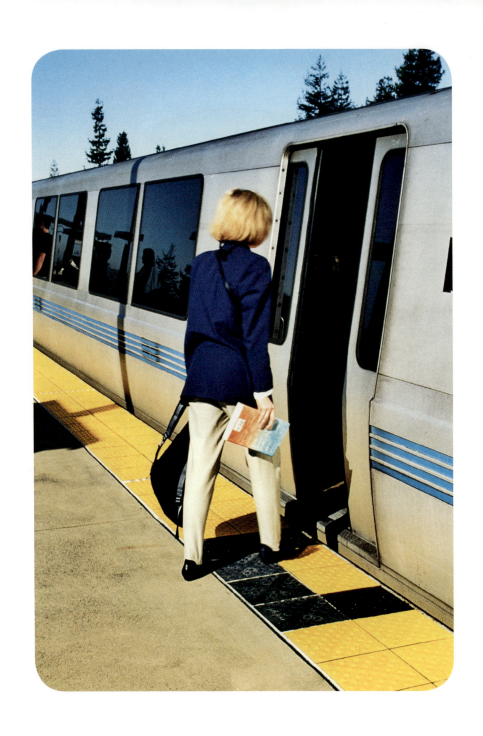

I see a train.

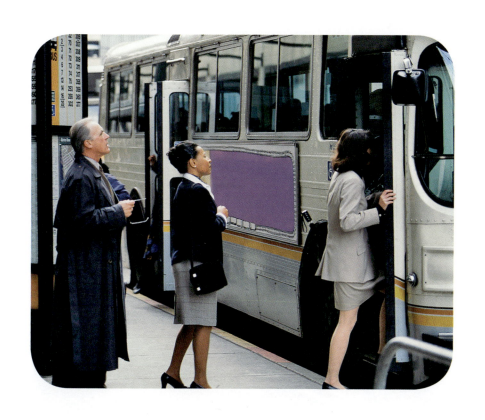

I see a bus.

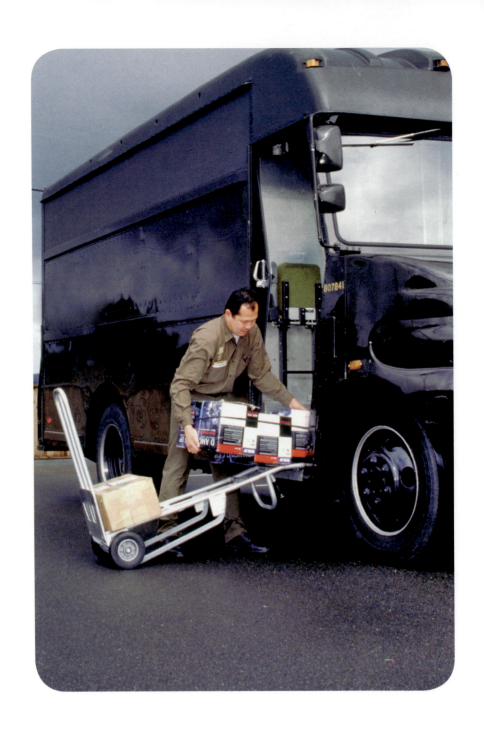

I see a truck.

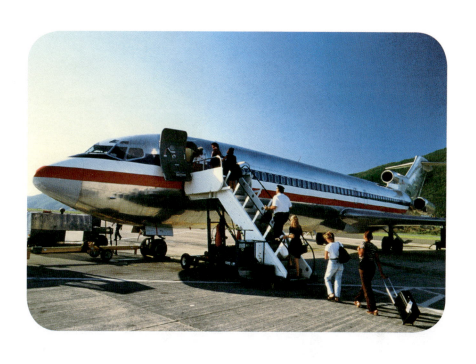

I see a plane.

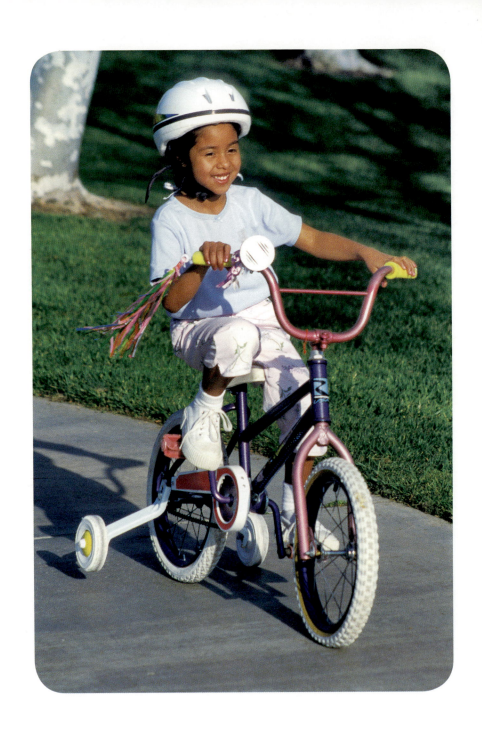

I see a bike.